Seven Wonders of
COMMUNICATION

Donald Cleveland

TWENTY-FIRST CENTURY BOOKS

Minneapolis

To Ana D. Cleveland—
you are always there when I need you!

Twenty-First Century Books
A division of Lerner Publishing Group, Inc.
241 First Avenue North
Minneapolis, MN 55401 U.S.A.

Website address: www.lernerbooks.com

Library of Congress Cataloging-in-Publication Data

Cleveland, Donald, 1935–
    Seven wonders of communication / by Donald Cleveland.
        p.   cm. — (Seven wonders)
    Includes bibliographical references and index.
    ISBN 978-0-7613-4240-3 (lib. bdg. : alk. paper)
    1. Telecommunication—Juvenile literature. 2. Multimedia communications—Juvenile literature. I. Title.
  TK5102.4.C554 2010
  621.382—dc22   2009020319

Manufactured in the United States of America
1 — DP — 12/15/09

Contents

INTRODUCTION

*P*EOPLE LOVE TO MAKE LISTS OF THE BIGGEST AND THE BEST. ALMOST TWENTY-FIVE HUNDRED YEARS AGO, A GREEK WRITER NAMED HERODOTUS MADE A LIST OF THE MOST AWESOME THINGS EVER BUILT BY PEOPLE. THE LIST INCLUDED BUILDINGS, STATUES, AND OTHER OBJECTS THAT WERE LARGE, WONDROUS, AND IMPRESSIVE. LATER, OTHER WRITERS ADDED NEW ITEMS TO THE LIST. WRITERS EVENTUALLY AGREED ON A FINAL LIST. IT WAS CALLED THE SEVEN WONDERS OF THE ANCIENT WORLD.

The list became so famous that people began imitating it. They made other lists of wonders. They listed the Seven Wonders of the Modern World and the Seven Wonders of the Middle Ages. People even made lists of undersea wonders. In these pages, you will find a list of Seven Wonders of Communication.

From the moment we are born, we try to communicate. We start by crying and flopping our arms and legs. Then we start gurgling. Before long we realize that people around us have funny noises coming out of their mouths and these noises mean something important. We try to make the same noises. Welcome to the wonders of communication.

WHAT IS COMMUNICATION?

Communication is the process by which most living things exchange information. In the 1940s, a mathematician named Claude E. Shannon gave us a picture of what communication is. His model became known as Shannon's Model of Communication. It looked like this:

Shannon's Basic Model of Communication

Communication source (Sender)	Encoder (Tool)	Channel (Physical medium)	Decoder (Platform)	Destination (Receiver)
→ message →	→ signal →	→ signal →	→ message →	

The communication source is where the information comes from. The information is then encoded. When someone talks or writes, that person's thoughts are "encoded" into language. The message then goes through a channel. In this case, the channel is air. At the receiving end, the message is decoded. If someone is talking or writing it, that person's brain decodes the language in order to understand it. The destination is the person receiving the message. Noise is anything that interferes with the communication process. Noise could be poor handwriting.

As we move through the following chapters on the Seven Wonders of Communication, keep Shannon's idea in mind. This is what communication is all about.

American mathematician Claude E. Shannon (left) created Shannon's Model of Communication.

1 THE INCREDIBLE
Human Language

These prehistoric cave paintings were found in a cave in Africa. Paintings from thousands of years ago help scientists discover how written language was developed.

$\mathcal{Y}$OU ARE ABLE TO READ THIS BOOK BECAUSE YOU HAVE THE GREATEST COMMUNICATION WONDER OF ALL TIMES IN YOUR HEAD. THIS IS HUMAN LANGUAGE. IT'S WHERE ALL THE WONDERS OF COMMUNICATION BEGIN.

Language can be spoken or written. Communicating vocally (speech) is a complicated process involving many parts of the body. Often speech includes body language such as jumping up and down and waving a fist.

Language can also be written. This allows us to communicate across distance and time. American author Mark Twain wrote in the nineteenth century about the adventures of Tom Sawyer and Huckleberry Finn. Hundreds of years in the future, people will read what he wrote, perhaps even citizens from other planets.

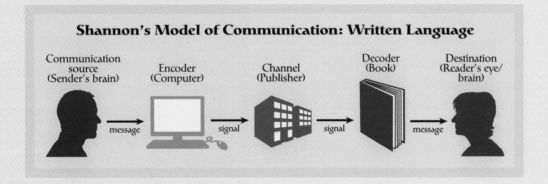

Shannon's Model of Communication: Written Language

Communication source (Sender's brain) → message → Encoder (Computer) → signal → Channel (Publisher) → signal → Decoder (Book) → message → Destination (Reader's eye/brain)

Language is nature's communication system for humans. It is a perfect example of Shannon's communication model. The author of this book is a source. My brain encoded my thoughts into language. I entered them into my computer. The channel in this case is the publisher of the book. My messages passed through a lot of people before becoming a book. Finally, someone opened the book and began to read. Word by word, a brain decoded the language.

This process allows me to share my thoughts. In the Shannon model, I am the source, and the reader is the destination. Language is the communication tool we both use to communicate.

ORIGINS OF LANGUAGE

No one knows for sure how language developed. Most scholars believe it developed along with the evolution of humans. No caveman woke up one morning and said, "Today I am going to invent talking." As humans evolved, their brains developed the abilities to acquire language. At the same time, sound-making parts developed in their throats and mouths.

While the physical parts developed in humans, their social awareness grew. Humans realized that the better they communicated with one another, the more successful they would be.

WHO IS *Noam Chomsky?*

Linguistics is the scientific study of language. Linguists are people who study the origins, rules, and workings of language. Noam Chomsky *(above)* is a famous linguist. In the 1950s, he pioneered new thinking about how people acquire language. Chomsky says we are born with the ability to learn a language. This ability works the same way for everybody. It makes no difference if the language is English, Spanish, or something else.

HUMAN SPEECH *Mechanisms*

The mouth and throat are for more than eating. Nearly one hundred muscles in the lungs, throat, mouth, and nasal cavity are used to produce human speech.

All these organs and body tissues contribute to making the sounds and words of speech.

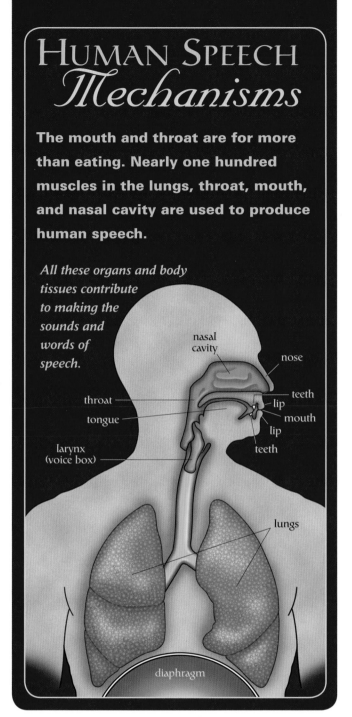

nasal cavity

nose

teeth

lip

mouth

lip

teeth

throat

tongue

larynx (voice box)

lungs

diaphragm

HOW LANGUAGE WORKS

A language begins with sounds and symbols. The basic unit is the word. A word is a string of sounds or symbols. Individual words have specific meanings. Real language begins when people string words together.

A language can string words together in thousands of different ways. Each way has to follow certain rules to be understood. Grammar is the set of rules for correctly speaking and writing a language. Syntax is a part of grammar. The rules of syntax determine the way words are strung together in a sentence. Semantics is the meaning of the words. For example, *bear* may mean "to put up with something unpleasant." But *bear* may also mean "a big, hairy animal."

PHYSICAL MECHANISMS OF HUMAN SPEECH

The physical act of speaking requires the exact coordination of a number of body parts. All of them are commanded by the brain. Neuroanatomists are scientists who study what different parts of the brain do. They have discovered what parts of the brain control speech.

Speech requires at least one hundred different muscles working as a team. The team follows orders from regions of the brain. The process begins with the lungs expelling air. This air passes through an organ in the throat called the larynx. The larynx changes the size and shape of its opening to make different sounds as the air passes through it. The shape determines if the sound is high-pitched, low-pitched, hard, or soft. The lips, tongue, teeth, and jaw put the final touch on the sound to get the words just right.

THE INVENTION OF WRITTEN LANGUAGE

The dawn of graphic (written) communication began more than thirty-two thousand years ago when prehistoric humans drew pictures and paintings on cave walls. Explorers have found these caves in Spain, France, Great Britain, and other countries.

Over time, small pictures began to represent words. A picture of a snake meant the word *snake*. From this, the ancient Egyptians invented a form of writing called hieroglyphics. A string of pictures expressed a complete thought. A long string of hieroglyphics might tell a story.

The Sumerians and Babylonians, in what is modern-day Iraq, started using wedge-shaped characters that stood for speech sounds. We call this cuneiform writing. Writers placed the cuneiforms in a certain order to mean certain ideas. Strings of cuneiforms resemble our present-day sentences. Cuneiform

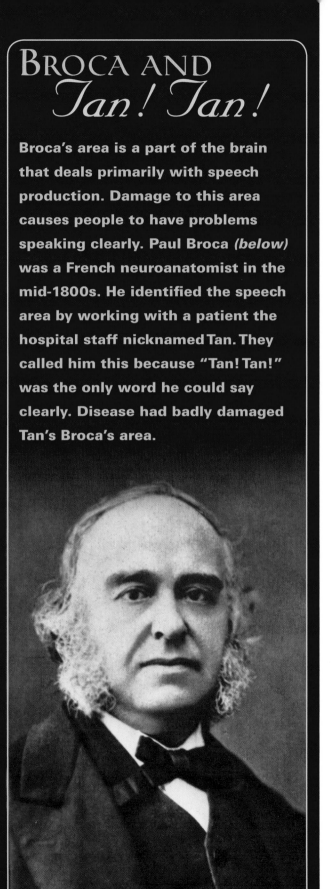

BROCA AND *Tan! Tan!*

Broca's area is a part of the brain that deals primarily with speech production. Damage to this area causes people to have problems speaking clearly. Paul Broca (below) was a French neuroanatomist in the mid-1800s. He identified the speech area by working with a patient the hospital staff nicknamed Tan. They called him this because "Tan! Tan!" was the only word he could say clearly. Disease had badly damaged Tan's Broca's area.

writing was a major step toward the invention of modern alphabets. As the years passed, alphabets developed in many forms all over the world.

To write, there has to be something to write on and to write with. Early humans wrote on rocks, wood, skins, and cloth. Ancient Egyptians pressed out papyrus plants to make a paperlike writing material. In A.D. 104 in China, a man named Tsai Lun invented paper made out of wood fiber. Over the centuries, this became the most common writing material.

Early people wrote with sharpened stones, bones, or sticks dipped in dye or some other colored liquid. The Greeks introduced the earliest writing tool similar to a pen. It was a stylus made of metal, bone, or ivory. Quill pens appeared around A.D. 700. Writers made quill pens by sharpening the ends

These hieroglyphics were found in a temple in Egypt. Ancient peoples used a series of pictures to tell a story or give information.

> *"When we study human language, we are approaching what some might call the 'human essence,' the . . . qualities of mind that are, so far as we know, unique to man."*
>
> —Noam Chomsky, 2006

of bird feathers. The feathers of geese, hawks, owls, and turkeys made the best pens.

The first fountain pen appeared in the mid-tenth century. The caliph (ruler) of Egypt ordered his staff to invent a writing tool that would hold ink and feed it to the writing tip. Gravity pulled the ink down from a storage area. When the storage area ran dry, the writer added more ink to it. The following centuries brought various improvements on the fountain pen.

This painting by a Spanish artist shows a priest using a quill pen. The painting is from the seventeenth century.

In 1500 the English invented pencils. In 1938 a Hungarian editor named Laszlo Biro made the first ballpoint pen. It was not as messy as a fountain pen. And it didn't need to be refilled.

Written language was a remarkable achievement. Equally remarkable is our modern ability to capture and preserve spoken language through technology, such as recordings. Together, written language and recorded spoken language will make our thoughts and reflections of life available for as long as the world exists.

PRINTING

The invention of the printing press changed communication. In the eleventh century, in China, a man named Bi Sheng invented a movable type device made of wood. In the thirteenth century, the Koreans invented a movable type device made of metal.

Movable type allows the printer to move letters around and reuse them. Before this invention, a printer had to carve all the letters and words for a page or group of pages from a single block of wood. The printer made copies, but the wood soon wore out, and new blocks had to be carved. It took a long time to print anything, and few copies could be made. To print another book, the printer had to carve other pages. Movable metal letters changed that.

"What gunpowder did for war, the printing press has done for the mind."

—Wendell Phillips, Boston lawyer, 1863

We give credit to a German, Johannes Gutenberg, for inventing a movable type printing press for the Western world in about 1450. His most famous printed work was the Gutenberg Bible.

Human communication changed in the years after Gutenberg. His press provided many inexpensive copies of books. This meant that the written word could be spread around the world. Having books available made people everywhere want to read.

WONDERS OF LANGUAGE

One of the real wonders of language is that it is forever changing. It changes to reflect the world around us and the world in our heads. We adjust our language to communicate better. Language is alive and strong. Many new words will appear in this century. Many other words will become outdated. Will there ever be a universal language? One language for everyone? Who knows?

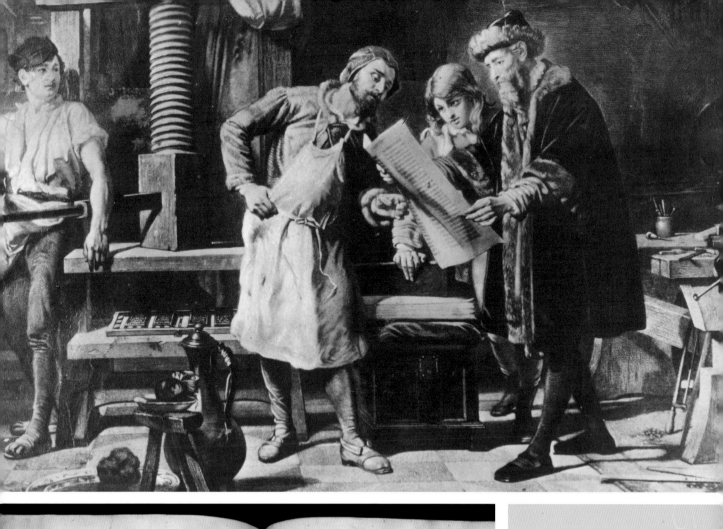

Top: *In this painting, Johannes Gutenberg examines a page off the first printing press in the mid-1400s.* Left: *These pages are from a Gutenberg Bible printed in 1455.*

2 Telephones Then and Now

These telephone operators direct calls in the early 1900s.

$\mathcal{Y}$OUR FRIEND IS ON VACATION AND IS STANDING ON THE GREAT WALL OF CHINA. YOU FLIP OPEN THE LITTLE DEVICE IN YOUR HAND. YOU SCROLL QUICKLY TO A FAMILIAR NUMBER. YOU PUSH A BUTTON. YOU HEAR SOME BUZZING, A CLICK OR TWO. IN A FEW SECONDS, YOUR FRIEND SAYS, "HEY, THERE!" FROM 12,000 MILES (19,312 KILOMETERS) AWAY. WELCOME TO THE WONDERS OF THE TELEPHONE.

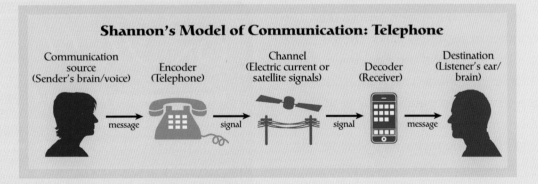

Shannon's Model of Communication: Telephone

Communication source (Sender's brain/voice) → message → Encoder (Telephone) → signal → Channel (Electric current or satellite signals) → signal → Decoder (Receiver) → message → Destination (Listener's ear/brain)

IT HAS A SYSTEM

Modern phones are part of an incredible communication system. It begins with the telephone in your hand. The phone is an electronic tool that encodes your voice, text message, or images into an electrical current. The current moves through a wire or a radio to a receiving phone.

Telephone systems connect phones into networks to make them useful. These systems carry thousands of conversations at the same time. The wonder is how the system manages to get so many messages from senders to receivers with such great reliability and clarity.

When you make a call, the computer in the system checks the number to see if it is valid. Then it figures out the location of the equipment that handles the phone you want to talk to. It alerts the computer in charge at that location. The computer at the receiving end causes the receiving phone to ring.

Someone answering the phone causes the computers on both ends to open up a circuit channel between the two phones. You have your own private channel in the system. When you turn off the phone, the computers shut down the channel.

Alexander Graham Bell (right front) *makes the first call on the New York to Chicago telecommunications service in 1892. Bell invented the telephone in 1876.*

ON *Hold*

The inventor of the phone, Alexander Graham Bell, and his assistant, Thomas Watson, were working on improving the phone. Bell was talking on the phone when someone asked to talk with him. Bell handed the phone to Watson and said, "Hold this," while he went to another room. Thus was born the term "putting someone on hold."

How Telephones Work

Telephones convert sound to electrical current and send the current to a receiving phone. The receiving phone converts the electrical current back into sound. Early phones had a mouthpiece containing a thin metal plate that vibrated in sync with the sound waves spoken into the phone mouthpiece. The thin plate was like an eardrum.

Female telephone operators work at the National Telephone Company in 1900.

All Done by Hand

Early phone systems were exchanges operated by people sitting in front of switchboards. They answered calls and plugged and unplugged wires to connect customers. In the beginning, these operators were boys. The boys were often rude to customers, so the phone exchanges replaced them with young women. The young women were more polite. In 1891 Almon B. Strowger invented an automatic telephone exchange. His company installed one in Kansas City, Missouri. Still, manual systems remained in use for decades more.

"The great advantage [the phone] possesses over every other form of electrical apparatus consists in the fact that it requires no skill to operate the instrument."

—Alexander Graham Bell, 1876

The vibrations of the plate caused electrical current to vary in strength and wavelength to reflect the changing sound waves.

Sound waves are invisible movements caused by vibrations. The sound wave vibrations push their way through air or another medium. Fast vibrations cause you to hear high-pitch sounds. Slow vibrations cause you to hear low-pitch sounds.

The telephone converted sound waves into electrical current. The electrical current then sped along through a wire to the other phone. At the receiving end, the process went into reverse. The incoming current caused a metal plate in the earpiece to vibrate. The vibrating thin metal plate produced sound waves that the human ear could pick up.

These early telephones worked by what is called an analog process. The analog process used the characteristics of the sound to convert it to an electrical current that has a similar pattern. When the sound changes, the electrical current changes. For example, if the sound rises in pitch or tone, the electrical current changes the same way. The patterns in the electrical current are an analog of the patterns in the sounds.

FROM ANALOG TO DIGITAL

Electronic communication devices still depend on the basic principle of converting sounds into electrical pulses at the sending end. Then they convert them back to sound at the receiving end. A new way of doing this is called digital processing.

With digital processing, zeros and ones represent the patterns of the sound waves, text, or images. A very large set of zeros and ones record the patterns. For sound, a specific set of zeros and ones represent the specific characteristics of sound, such as pitch. The receiving computer reads the sets of zeros and ones. It reproduces them as sounds in its speakers.

MANY
Inventors

Many different people worked on developing the telephone. One of these inventors, Elisha Gray, actually developed a telephone about the same time as Bell. But Bell beat him by a few hours in filing for a patent for it. The famous genius inventor Thomas A. Edison also worked on developing the telephone, such as the one at left.

Telephones have gone through dozens of style and technical changes. In the 1920s, telephones had separate hearing and speaking pieces (middle left). Later that decade, telephones with one handpiece for both listening and speaking were introduced (middle right). Phones had rotary dials for making calls for many decades. In the 1970s, touch-tone dialing was introduced. And modern phones have a touch-tone keypad, as well as answering machines and cordless receivers (bottom left).

Telephones and phone systems are moving into a digital world because digital technology has better voice quality and less noise. Digital technology has more ways for transmitting and receiving. For example, modern technology squeezes digital signals into a smaller space. This allows many more phone signals to be sent at the same time over a single channel. Analog signals use a lot of space in a channel.

CELL PHONES

The cell phone in your backpack is really a radio. It is a powerful radio with a small transmitter, receiver, microphone, speaker, antenna, and battery. Cell phones can be either analog or digital, though most new ones are digital. Either way, they work in a similar way:

- The phone translates your messages into an electrical current.
- The radio transmitter in the phone sends the current over the air as a radio signal.
- The radio receiver in the receiving phone accepts the incoming radio signal.
- The receiving phone converts the received signal into messages that humans recognize.

FUN FACT: *No Sound*

The moon has no air or water. Therefore, there is no sound on the moon. There is nothing for the sound waves to move through. Also, to have sound, something must hear the sound—such as your ears.

The cellular batteries used in cell phones were developed in the 1940s. But it wasn't until 1983 that the Federal Communications Commission, a government agency, approved the first mobile phone for use in the United States.

Left: *This cellular communications tower allows users to send and receive cell phone signals.* **Right:** *This modern cell phone tower is disguised as a palm tree.*

Cell phones use cell sites to help send messages. Towers at the cell sites are equipped with many big antennas. When you call your friend standing on the Great Wall of China, your cell signal hops from antenna to antenna. Communication companies have placed cell sites all around the world. Usually, these sites are 20 to 30 miles (32 to 48 km) apart. If your cell signal is traveling

"I have always wished that my computer would be as easy to use as my telephone. My wish has come true. I no longer know how to use my telephone."
—*Bjarne Stronstrup, computer scientist at Bell Labs, 1979*

long distances, it probably goes by way of communication satellites in orbit around Earth. Finally, the signal ends up at a local cell site near the Great Wall. Your friend hears his phone ring—or feels it vibrate.

Cell phones are used all over the world. An organization called the Wireless Association says that in 2008 the United States had 263 million

Communications satellites, like this one, orbit Earth and receive and send signals to many communication devices, including cell phones.

TRAFFIC JAM
in the Sky

Satellites are objects placed into orbit around Earth. They play a big role in modern communication. Many government or private groups have put thousands of satellites in the sky. Some have died out and have become sky junk. New ones go up all the time. Communication satellites:

- **Reflect or relay radio signals**
- **Connect to locations on the ground and in the air with built-in radio equipment**
- **Act as switchboards for communication**
- **Carry more than half of all long-distance telephone calls**
- **Carry TV broadcasts**
- **Provide military communications**
- **Help with Internet connections**

Newer cell phones, like this iPhone from Apple, are multimedia centers. They allow the user to not only talk on the phone but to also connect to the Internet, listen to music, and watch videos.

cell phone customers. Millions and millions more cell phones are in service around the world.

WONDERS TO COME

If Alexander Graham Bell were still around, his jaw would drop in surprise at what has happened to the telephone he invented in 1876. We are entering the 3G age of telephones. The term "3G" means "the third generation of phone technology and networking."

Global systems connect phones with blazing speeds. Cell phones can hold large amounts of information. They have access to music, videos, TV, and the Internet. They are multimedia centers, where everything is connected and accessible. All communication tools are coming together on the phone. Since their beginning, telephones have been a wonder of communication, and many wonders are still ahead.

3 Cameras—FROM BLACK BOX TO DIGITAL

A man takes a photograph outdoors in 1911.

COMMUNICATION IS NOT JUST ABOUT OUR MOUTH AND EARS. IT IS ALSO ABOUT WHAT WE SEE. OF COURSE, WHEN WE READ, WE ARE SEEING LANGUAGE ON PAPER. BUT COMMUNICATION WITH IMAGES GOES MUCH FURTHER THAN THIS. IMAGES COMMUNICATE IDEAS, INFORMATION, AND EMOTIONS. THESE IMAGES COME TO US THROUGH PICTURES IN BOOKS, THROUGH COMPUTERS, AND THROUGH TV.

Images all around us give out information. Little pictures of men and women even help us get into the correct public restroom! Drawing and painting are great communicators, but probably the most powerful visual communicator of all is the camera. There are cameras everywhere. Everybody seems to have one. Cameras allow powerful visual communication. They are a wonder of communication.

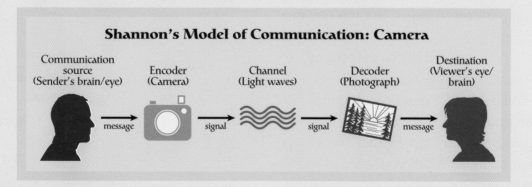

Shannon's Model of Communication: Camera

Communication source (Sender's brain/eye) → message → Encoder (Camera) → signal → Channel (Light waves) → signal → Decoder (Photograph) → message → Destination (Viewer's eye/brain)

How Cameras Work

Cameras use light to make images of real things. Light carries information, such as shapes, shadows, and colors that will create an image. The light enters a camera through the lens—a curved piece of glass or plastic at the front of the camera.

When the picture taker presses a button, the shutter opens. The shutter is a kind of door that opens and closes to control the amount of time the light passes through the lens. The aperture is an opening that can be made larger or smaller to control how much light enters through the lens. The light entering the lens falls on film. The light causes chemical changes in the film that makes the image.

A digital camera also uses light to create images but uses no film. The upfront operations of digital cameras and film cameras are pretty much the same. They have a lens, shutter, aperture, and buttons to click. But the digital camera has a microprocessor, like the one in a computer.

A part of the digital camera called a sensor receives the light. It captures the light details that describe the photographed object. It saves these details the way a computer saves information. When you want to see the picture, the digital camera converts the information into images that your eyes and brain recognize.

Traditional film cameras (below) *have mostly been replaced by digital point-and-shoot cameras* (bottom), *as well as more complex digital single-lens cameras.*

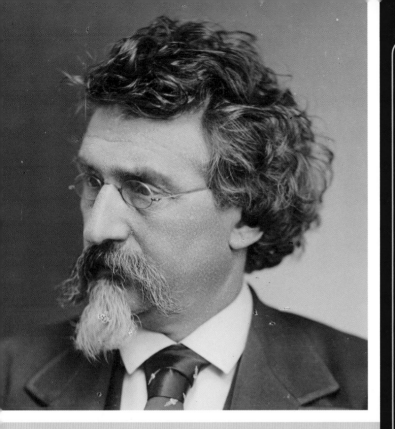

WHO WAS *Mathew Brady?*

Historians call Mathew Brady *(left)* the father of photojournalism, telling news stories in photos. He is best remembered for his many photo images of Civil War battlefields. He would drive his photo lab wagon right into the battles and set up to take pictures. He also photographed eighteen U.S. presidents, starting with John Quincy Adams in the 1820s and ending with William McKinley in the 1890s.

Below: *Mathew Brady's picture gallery is shown in this photo from the Civil War in the 1860s.*

PICTURES THAT MOVE

There is nothing magical about moving pictures. They are not really moving. A movie is a series of still pictures that pass very fast before a person's eyes.

When someone looks at an object and then turns away—or the object passes out of sight—an image of it lingers for a short moment in the brain. So when a series of pictures, each slightly changed, move across a person's vision, the brain blends the series of pictures. When the film shows twenty-four images per second, a viewer thinks he or she sees movement. It is really a trick played on the brain.

At the end of the nineteenth century, people first experimented with making moving pictures. These movies were short scenes showing some kind of movement, such as somebody opening and closing a window.

THE FIRST Cowboy Movie

The first film that told a story was *The Great Train Robbery* (shown above) in 1903. Although it was only twelve minutes long, people were fascinated. The film demonstrated that cameras could tell a story with characters and action.

The first real feature film was *The Great Train Robbery,* in 1903. It starred Bronco Billy Anderson. A feature film tells a complete story. It is more than just a collection of moving pictures strung together. People called these stories on film picture shows.

In 1928 Walt Disney produced a short animated film called *Steamboat Willie.* It starred Mickey Mouse. Disney became the animation leader of the world. He pioneered all kinds of special cameras and techniques for making cartoon movies.

Animated films work just like any movie. The difference is that the pictures are drawn. They are not photos of real things. Each drawing has a very slight change. Twenty-four drawings are needed for each second of viewing. The drawings are spliced together into a long film.

Seven Wonders of Communication

How *Photocopying Works*

A photocopier is a special kind of camera. Light projects a page or picture onto a drum inside the photocopier. The drum is made of material that will change the projected image into an electrical current. A powdery substance called a toner covers the drum. The toner on the drum reacts with the electrical current. The current causes the grains of toner on the drum to arrange themselves into a mirror image of the page or picture. The drum rolls across a blank sheet of paper, and the toner is pressed onto it in a copy of the page or image. The toner, which is like ink, quickly dries, and the machine spits out the copy.

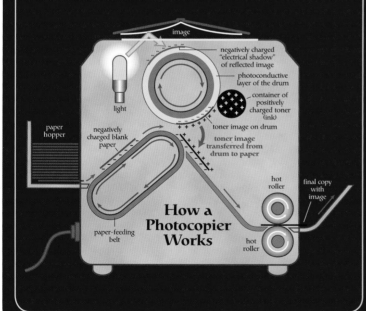

How a Photocopier Works

image

negatively charged "electrical shadow" of reflected image

photoconductive layer of the drum

container of positively charged toner (ink)

light

paper hopper

negatively charged blank paper

toner image on drum

toner image transferred from drum to paper

paper-feeding belt

hot roller

hot roller

final copy with image

That's a lot of drawings. Disney's famous animated movie, *Snow White and the Seven Dwarfs* (1937), required about 1.5 million drawings and paintings. Humans drew and painted each one. In modern times, computers make and color many of the drawings.

An important event occurred in 1927. Warner Brothers studios made a movie called *The Jazz Singer*. It starred Al Jolson. It was the first feature movie with sound. That meant that pictures not only could move, they could talk—and sing.

Moviemaking technology developed rapidly after this. In the 1930s and 1940s, theaters sprang up in every corner of the country. Kids could go to the picture show for as little as fifteen cents. A bag of popcorn cost a nickel.

CAMERAS IN SCIENCE AND TECHNOLOGY

It would be difficult to find any area of science and technology that doesn't use cameras. Cameras plus computers make a very powerful communication tool for scientists and technicians.

Cameras have a wide range of uses in biology. Scientists connect cameras to microscopes. They take sharp, clear pictures of the smallest living things, even the inner workings of cells. Cameras go into the forest and under the sea to capture the lives and habitats of animals.

Exploration rockets pass by planets taking pictures. Rovers land on the planets and roll around taking pictures. For example, the *Phoenix* Mars Lander landed on Mars on May 25, 2008. It had two cameras. One camera was on a robotic arm just above a scoop that digs soil. The camera took close-up pictures of the ground and soil samples. The other camera was set on top of the *Phoenix* It took three-dimensional views of the arctic plains of Mars. On November 2, 2008, the National Aeronautics and Space Administration (NASA) reported that communication with the *Phoenix* had stopped. The *Phoenix* Mars Lander cameras had taken great pictures for five months.

All kinds of cameras are up in the sky. Some are on space shuttles. Some are on satellites. Some are on airplanes. These cameras include weather cameras, spy cameras, and land use cameras. Land use cameras study water, glaciers, soil, forests, cities, effects of pollution, and hundreds of other things. Cameras above Earth help in mapmaking. They work with other satellite

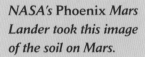

NASA's **Phoenix** *Mars Lander took this image of the soil on Mars.*

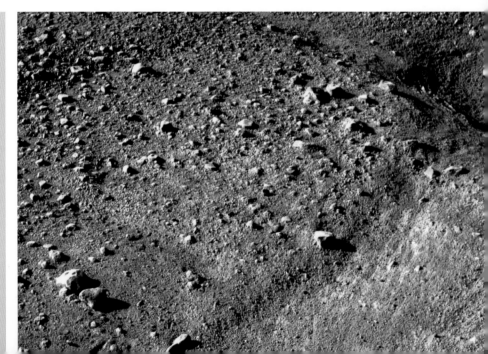

This global positioning system (GPS) in a vehicle uses satellites to help travelers pinpoint their location.

devices, such as global positioning systems (GPS). This satellite system locates objects on Earth and can even track their movements.

Cameras also look into the very heart of the galaxy and beyond. Some of these cameras are in telescopes on the ground, and others are in telescopes orbiting Earth.

Actors take pictures of the crime scene on almost every TV crime show. This happens in real life too, when police use cameras in detective work.

Live TV cameras and video recorders surround us in public places. They are placed and monitored in malls, stores, schools, and dozens of other sites to provide safety.

Medical imaging is the technology and techniques for looking inside humans. It combines cameras, X-ray machines, computers, and other devices to make images of the inside of the body. These images help diagnose diseases.

VISUAL *Persuasion*

Advertising is a multibillion dollar business, and visual images are at the heart of it. Ads appear on TV, on the World Wide Web, and in all kinds of print media. Images appear in almost all commercials and advertisements. Advertising professionals call this visual persuasion. It works!

FUTURE WONDERS

Cameras keep evolving, taking new forms and opening new potentials. They have built-in communication links to other media and the Internet. Cameras have been around for less than two hundred years. They have had a tremendous impact on the way we see and understand the world. They allow us to record and preserve our history. They capture our lives for communication to future generations.

A family watches television in the 1950s. Television sets were first made available to the public in 1948.

*T*ELEVISION IS EVERYWHERE. THERE ARE MANY MILLIONS OF TV SETS ALL AROUND THE WORLD. MORE THAN 98 PERCENT OF THE HOUSEHOLDS IN THE UNITED STATES HAVE ONE TELEVISION SET. MORE THAN 90 PERCENT HAVE MORE THAN ONE. ONLY FARAWAY, REMOTE PLACES MAY NOT HAVE TV.

Some say TV promotes violence and loosens morals. They complain that TV makes people lazy couch potatoes. It makes them buy things they don't need. Some say TV makes viewers fat because they snack while they watch TV, while the commercials encourage them to buy junk food.

Others see TV as entertaining and educational. They point out that viewers learn many things from TV that they may never have the chance to experience in person. TV viewers see the glaciers of Antarctica and watch the penguins wobble across the ice. They look out the window of a space shuttle at the blue green ball called Earth. This is all through the wonders of television.

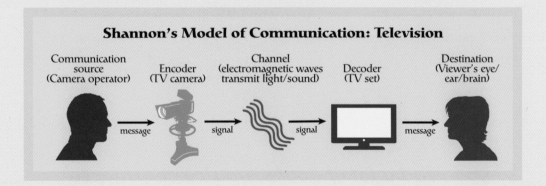

Shannon's Model of Communication: Television

Communication source (Camera operator) — message → Encoder (TV camera) — signal → Channel (electromagnetic waves transmit light/sound) — signal → Decoder (TV set) — message → Destination (Viewer's eye/ear/brain)

THE MANY INVENTORS OF TELEVISION

Many people worked on the technology that developed television. In the late 1890s, Guglielmo Marconi first demonstrated workable radio communication. Radio waves traveled through the air, without any wires. Radio developed quickly. In the early 1900s, scientists and engineers began to wonder if they could send pictures through the air as well as sounds.

In April 1927, AT&T research laboratories first sent a television transmission between New York City and Washington, D.C. The British were also working on developing TV. On May 12, 1937, they broadcast the ceremonies when George VI became king. From 1936 to 1939, the British Broadcasting Corporation presented television programming for about four hours a day. Britons living in London owned close to fifteen thousand television sets. TV broadcasts stopped when World War II (1939–1945) started.

The first U.S. president to be televised was Franklin D. Roosevelt. It was at the 1939 World's Fair in New York. After World War II, researchers resumed their work on developing commercial TV. In 1948 TV sets became available to the general public.

Guglielmo Marconi, shown here in the early 1900s, was an Italian inventor. He is credited with first developing radio.

"If you read a lot of books, you're considered well-read. But if you watch a lot of TV, you're not considered well-viewed."

—*Lily Tomlin, actress, comedian, writer, and producer, 1977*

How Television Works

Television sends and receives sights and sounds using invisible waves. Nature surrounds us with these waves. These are not ocean waves or the greeting from a friend across the room. These waves are unseen energy disturbances that move through the air. They include the sound waves created when people talk—or when a firecracker pops.

The Long and Short of *Electromagnetic Waves*

Electromagnetic waves of different lengths have different functions. They can do different things according to how long they are. Each wave has a wavelength. It is the distance between one wave crest to the next. Radio waves are the longest. If we put wavelengths in order of length from long to short, the order is:

- Radio waves (radios and TVs)
- Microwaves (cooks a hot dog)
- Infrared (heat that can't be seen except with special goggles)
- Visible spectrum (colors that can be seen: red, yellow, orange, green, blue, and violet)
- Ultraviolet rays (invisible but can cause you sunburn)
- X-rays (strong enough to pierce a body and take pictures inside)
- Gamma rays (advanced medical imaging machines use these)

Electromagnetic waves are a type of wave related to electricity and magnetism. These waves make radios work. They also make TVs, TV remote controls, cell phones, microwave ovens, garage door openers, and many other things work.

Electromagnetic waves consist of an electrical field and a magnetic field. An electrical current gives off an electrical field. This might be the electricity in a wall socket or a battery. A magnetic field makes things attract one another, such as a little magnet and a refrigerator door.

When an electrical field and a magnetic field join, the result is an electromagnetic wave. The waves vibrate and transfer energy. A microphone and a transmitter impose sound waves onto electromagnet waves to send out a radio broadcast.

"If it weren't for the fact that the TV set and the refrigerator are so far apart, some of us wouldn't get any exercise at all."

—*Joey Adams, comedian, n. d.*

Wave frequency is a measure of how many waves come out of a transmitter over a fixed period of time. The Federal Communications Commission, a government agency, assigns each television station its own frequency. This allows stations to broadcast at the same time over their different frequencies.

The TV process is another example of Shannon's communication model. The steps for TV broadcasting are:

- A TV camera takes a series of pictures of the scene. A microphone picks up the sound.
- The TV camera takes twenty-four pictures a second. A scanner passes over each picture. It divides the image into about 575 lines and quickly scans it line by line to convert it into an electrical current.
- A TV transmitter converts the electrical version of the pictures into electromagnetic waves and sends them and the related sounds out over the air.
- A TV receiver picks up the electromagnetic waves and converts them back into pictures and sound that come out of the TV set.

This television camera is taking pictures of a news broadcaster. This is just the first step in sending TV signals to your home TV set.

With computers and cell phones, people can now get their visual images from many different sources, not just the television.

THE SOCIAL AND ECONOMIC IMPACT OF TELEVISION

Television has grown to be the most popular communication medium of all times. It is a force in the lives of people everywhere. Almost every day somebody talks about a TV program or says, "I saw on TV last night that . . ." Humans created television, and television creates them, as well.

Some believe that people learn how to act in life by what they see and hear on TV. They tend to buy things they see on TV. People get the news from TV. Many people turn on the set the first thing when they get home.

Television promotes our culture, to ourselves and to other people. Viewers learn about these

TELEVISION AND *Advertising*

Companies and other groups will spend large amounts of money to run ads on TV to influence viewers. For example, TV advertising during the Super Bowl XLIII football game in 2009 cost about $3 million for thirty seconds.

During the presidential campaign, candidate Barack Obama is shown on a wall of television sets at a store in Virginia in October 2008. Many people learn about political candidates by watching programs and advertisements on television.

other cultures, as well. What they learn about faraway places and people may make them decide to explore further.

Politics and television go hand in hand. In the early days of TV, politicians were uneasy about appearing on television. They were afraid people would find out things about them that they didn't want the public to know. That attitude changed quickly. Modern politicians scramble to get on talk shows. TV crews follow them everywhere they go.

Think about the last presidential election. There were televised debates, political experts talking on the TV screen, hundreds of little background stories on the candidates and their families, and endless political advertisements. At last, Election Day arrived. Millions of people watched TV to see who would win.

> *"I find television to be very educating. Every time somebody turns on the set, I go in the other room and read a book."*
>
> —Groucho Marx, actor and comedian, n.d.

FUTURE WONDERS

In 2009 TV broadcasting went digital. Federal law required that all TV stations in the United States broadcast only in a digital format. TV had always been transmitted in the analog format. In the 1990s, engineers developed digital TV broadcasting and reception.

In 2009 people who wanted to continue using their old analog TV set had to buy a converter box. The box changes the incoming digital TV signal into an analog format so people can watch with their old set. If they received TV by cable or satellite, they didn't have to worry about it. The service providers change the signals to analog for old TVs.

Cell phone networks and the Internet are changing the way people view TV. Viewers can watch their favorite programs on their own schedule. Smart cell phones access TV and videos. TV videos are available on the Internet from libraries and commercial sources all around the world. Laptops can receive TV for viewing in the office, on a ship, or at home. New software allows viewers to watch the first part of movies while the end is still downloading. In fact, viewers can rewind the first part while the last part is downloading.

TV is becoming part of a global communication package in powerful ways. Wonder what's on TV tonight? Grab the cell phone and find out.

Viewers can watch television programs in a variety of ways. Some cell phones, such as the one shown above, allow people to access TV shows. Many people watch television shows on their computers as well.

THE PERSONAL Computer

Three people at the University of Pennsylvania work with one of the first computers, Electronic Numerical Integrator and Computer (ENIAC). ENIAC was built in 1946.

*A*S NOTED IN THE FIRST CHAPTER, HUMAN LANGUAGE IS THE MOST POWERFUL EXAMPLE OF SHANNON'S COMMUNICATION MODEL IN TERMS OF NATURAL COMMUNICATION. PERHAPS THE MOST POWERFUL EXAMPLE OF HIS MODEL IN TERMS OF COMMUNICATION TECHNOLOGY IS THE COMPUTER. THIS IS ESPECIALLY TRUE OF THE PERSONAL COMPUTER.

Computers brought to the world a new and powerful communication tool. The development of the small personal computer made it possible for everybody to have one. The computer is one of the great wonders of communication technology.

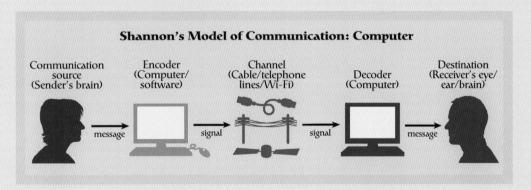

Shannon's Model of Communication: Computer

| Communication source (Sender's brain) | Encoder (Computer/ software) | Channel (Cable/telephone lines/Wi-Fi) | Decoder (Computer) | Destination (Receiver's eye/ ear/brain) |

message → signal → signal → message

Harvard University built the first modern computer in the early 1940s. Called Mark I, it was partly electronic and partly mechanical. It had relays, rotating metal parts, and clutches. Relays are electric switches that turn on and off according to a current sent to them from another switch. Clutches are devices for engaging or disengaging motors, pulleys, and other mechanical devices.

In 1946 engineers at the University of Pennsylvania built the first fully electronic computer. They named it the Electronic Numerical Integrator and Computer (ENIAC).

In the late 1950s, computers spread into the business world, mainly sold by International Business Machines (IBM) and Control Data Corporation (CDC).

Right: *Two men work on the Mark I at Harvard University in 1952.* **Below:** *The Mark I was the first modern computer. Once started, the computer could run on its own without human intervention. Mark I marked the beginning of the computer age.*

You've come a Long Way Baby

The 1946 ENIAC computer:

- Used 17,468 vacuum tubes for processing. It had limited storage. Storage holds all the computer programs and data that the computer needs to do its work.
- Weighed 27 tons (24 metric tons)
- Measured approximately 3 feet (1 meter) by 8.5 feet (2.6 m) by 80 feet (24 m)
- Used IBM punched cards for in putting information. Punched cards were made of stiff paper, about the size of a business envelope. The position and patterns of holes punched in the cards represented all numbers and all the letters in the alphabet. The computer understood what the holes meant.
- Used to do mathematical calculations

A Typical 2008 Personal Computer

- Uses microchips for processing with large amounts of storage
- Weighs a few pounds
- A typical laptop computer measures 10 by 8 inches (25 by 20 centimeters) and 1.5 inches (3.8 cm) thick
- Inputs with keyboard, disk drives, scanners, touch screens, and other devices
- Has dozens and dozens of functions, including text and image processing, searching the Internet, playing music, and much more

Computers have changed a lot since the 1940s. The ENIAC computer (above) *took up an entire room. Most modern computers easily fit on a desktop* (bottom).

THE INVENTION OF THE MICROCHIP

The computers of the 1960s were very useful. But they were big and took up great amounts of space. They gave off a lot of heat, and they cost a lot of money. Only large organizations with large amounts of money could own computers.

Vacuum tubes were the basic technology for early computers. These tubes controlled the movement of electrons—tiny parts around the outside of an atom.

When you add energy, such as a battery, to certain materials, it sets off a reaction. Electrons from the new energy make the electrons in the atoms in the original material move over to make room for the new electrons. The first atoms push out electrons to the next atoms— and so on down the line. This becomes a flow of electrons, an electrical current. Electronic communication devices work by controlling this flow of electrons from one point to another.

VACUUM TUBES
Make Electrons Behave

Vacuum tubes:

- **Look like an electric lightbulb. They have a case of glass or light metal.**
- **Are a vacuum (have no air) inside. This aids in the flow of the electrons.**
- **Have a metal heating element called an emitter at the bottom**
- **Have a metal plate at the top**
- **May have grids in between. Grids are pieces of metal with coils of wire around them.**
- **Boil off electrons when the emitter heats up. Regulating the heat controls their flow. The plate at the top collects the electrons.**
- **Help control the electrons by means of the grids by keeping stray electrons from getting off course on their way to the plate**

Vacuum tubes are good for

- **Converting alternating current (AC) to direct current (DC). AC comes out of wall sockets. DC comes out of batteries. Electronic devices need DC current to do their work.**
- **Controlling the sounds in your communication devices. The grids can throw more electrons into the stream, and your radio gets louder. This is called amplification.**
- **Generating electromagnetic radio waves for radios and TVs**
- **Generating radar waves**

Vacuum tubes were powerful technology for their time, but they were large. The equipment that used them had to be large enough to house them.

In the late 1940s, transistors began to replace vacuum tubes. Producers make transistors out of a solid piece of material, such as germanium or silicon. These metals conduct electricity. Transistors do the same things as vacuum tubes. But they don't need to have a vacuum to work, so they are smaller. They use less electricity and are much cooler. They don't burn out as fast and cost a lot less. Transistors are a key element in most all modern electronics.

Then researchers invented microchips. Producers make microchips with a process known as photolithography. Light and chemicals etch the patterns on a small piece of material. Most often this material is a thin slice of silicon. A microchip seen under a microscope shows hundreds of interconnected regions. It looks like a street map of a large city.

These connections form tiny electrical circuits called integrated circuits. Electrical currents zip through the chip from one junction to another. The signals take different paths for different functions. The circuits can switch to many different pathways at a very high speed.

The microchip led to the development of the personal computer, and a whole new type of computer was born. The two types of microchips in computers are microprocessors and storage chips. Microprocessors are for computer logic. They tell the computer what to do. The other chips store information in the computer's memory.

Microchips, with their integrated circuits, travel with us everywhere we go. They are in cell phones, media players, cars, space shuttles and, of course, laptop computers. Chips may be one of the most important inventions in the history of technology. They help create a digital world.

WHO ARE *Jack Kilby* AND *Robert Noyce?*

Jack Kilby and Robert Noyce both came up with the idea of the integrated circuit (below). Kilby worked for Texas Instruments. Noyce founded his own company called Intel. In 2000 Kilby won a Nobel Prize for his work.

ENTER MICROCOMPUTERS

Microcomputers began as kits for hobbyists in the 1970s. It didn't take long for microcomputers to become more than toys. In 1975 IBM introduced a small

A Wonderful Piece of Plastic *in Its Time*

IBM invented the floppy disk *(below)* in the 1970s. This was a handy way to store extra information for small computers. Big computers used huge tape and disk drives. The floppy was a flat, round piece of plastic. A coat of magnetic material covered it. It was flexible, or floppy. The floppy was first an 8 inch (20 cm) disk. Later, manufacturers reduced it to 5.25 inches (13 cm) and then to 3.5 inches (8.9 cm). A square or rectangular envelope covered the disk to protect it. A small slot in the cover allowed the computer to write on or read the floppy as it spun by the open slot. For twenty years, the floppy was a major storage medium for small computers. The CD replaced it in the 1990s.

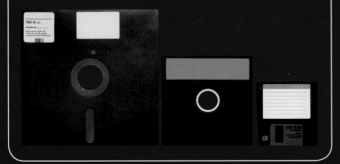

computer called the IBM 5100. This computer was expensive, beyond the reach of most people. Apple Computer sold the first truly personal computer (PC). It wasn't as expensive as the IBM, and it was easy to use.

In the beginning, the information processed by large computers came printed on long sheets of paper. The early personal computers also used paper printouts, but Apple and IBM also developed computers with monitors.

The TRS-80 from Radio Shack had a separate video monitor. The great advantage for the TRS-80 was that Radio Shack had stores almost everywhere, and this allowed them to sell computers on a large scale.

Other electronics companies created other models. IBM then came out with a more practical small computer called the IBM PC. When people thought about a personal computer, they usually meant the IBM machine.

Software Is the Secret

The computer programs that run computers are called software. There are two broad types of

Microsoft founder Bill Gates sits with a variety of computers in the early 1980s. Developing software for personal computers set off the PC revolution.

software—system software and application software. System software actually runs the computer. It accepts information and turns it over to other software for processing. Then it orders the computer to output information to a monitor, printer, or storage device. It might also send it off to another location through a network.

Application software does the needed work. This could be word processing, playing a video, or improving pictures from a digital camera.

The microcomputers couldn't use the large, complicated software developed for big computers. Bill Gates of Microsoft, as well as other companies, began to develop software for personal computers. New, powerful software brought a rapid growth of PCs in business, in education, and in the home. People everywhere began to have their own computer. The PC revolution had begun.

"When the PC was launched, people knew it was important."

—Bill Gates, founder of Microsoft Corporation, 2001

TYPES OF PERSONAL *Computers*

PCs come in many different forms. Some examples:

- **Desktops** are the regular computers we see on people's desks everywhere.
- **Laptops** are fully functional, powerful computers, about the size of a briefcase. In the beginning, they were heavy and a little bulky. But they are becoming lighter and more portable.
- **Pocket PC/personal digital assistants (PDAs)** are sometimes called a palmtop. They are very small and at first had simple applications, such as appointment calendars, calculators, and address books. It is an electronic version of the little paper notebooks that people carried in their shirt pockets and purses. The PDA later evolved into more powerful devices, such as smart phones. These are cell phones with computers inside. They allow full Internet access and a lot of computing capabilities.
- **Tablet PCs** look like writing pads, except they are metal with a screen. They have a keyboard and a metal pencil.
- **Portable multimedia players** are carry-around devices for storing and playing digital media, including audio, images, and video games.

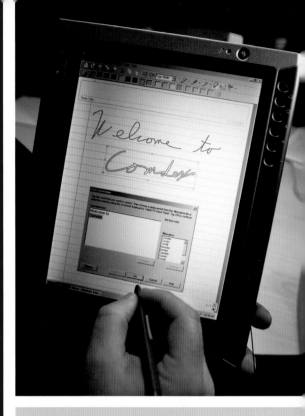

Popular PCs include tablet PCs (above); portable media players, such as this iPod (bottom far left); laptop computers; and PDAs (both pictured below).

When Our PCs Are Violated

Some computer experts and criminals can enter computers to cause problems. The most common invaders include viruses, which are electronic "germs" that attach themselves to the computer's programs. When the computer programs open, the germs damage hardware, programs, and data.

A worm is a special kind of virus. It copies itself from one computer to another, sometimes all around the world.

Spyware is software that sneaks in from other computers and gathers personal information from a person's computer. Spies sell the information to advertisers, and the buyer might suddenly slam an advertisement, called a pop-up, on a person's computer screen.

Hackers are people who get into files and copy personal information about a person's life or about finances. They might use the information to steal from that person. Hackers don't always do harm. But they can be annoying!

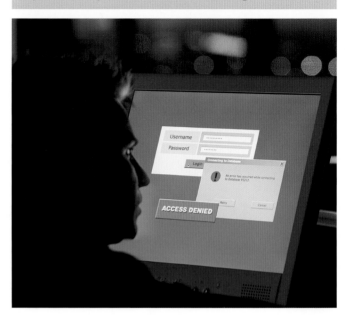

Hackers sometimes try to get personal information from a person's computer. They can use this information to do harm, such as stealing.

Future Wonders

Personal computers of the future will take new forms and have more functions. PCs will connect to everything. Most important, they will have fantastic power because of new computing technology, called nanotechnology. Nanotechnology works at the atomic and molecular levels. This way, it can develop ever smaller materials and processes.

Scientists and engineers are looking into ways to make deoxyribonucleic acid (DNA) do calculations. These "biochips" will be able do the same operations as microchips. The biochip technique changes the structure of the DNA molecules to represent information for the computer. When another computer looks at the molecule's structure, it understands the information

This biochip is used to quickly identify infectious disease strains.

that the structure represents. The scientists and engineers are sure biochips will work. Actually building a biochip computer though is a challenging task.

Another technology will create quantum computers, based on quantum mechanics. Quantum mechanics is the science of atomic structures and functions. It deals with what's going on inside an atom.

Quantum mechanics uses something called a qubit. A qubit is a basic unit of quantum information. It is similar to the zeros and ones stored on a microchip. The difference is a qubit can represent information between zero and one. There are an infinite number of values between a zero and one—such as, .1, .01, .001, all the way into infinity. Infinity goes on forever.

A qubit uses the electrical charge of the basic particles inside atoms to represent information. Information is stored inside the atoms of a material. The important thing is that this processing inside atoms allows a quantum computer to work on millions of computations at once. An ordinary PC works on one thing at a time.

Building quantum computers will not be easy. First, scientists and engineers need to solve many theoretical and practical problems. But quantum computers will come. They will be ten thousand times more powerful than modern computers. And they will store huge amounts of information in very small spaces.

The coming world of computers is about sharing information—sharing it with one another, to every point on Earth and beyond. Get ready. People will be walking around with the most powerful computer ever dreamed of in a pockets or backpacks—or embedded in their bodies.

THE World Wide Web

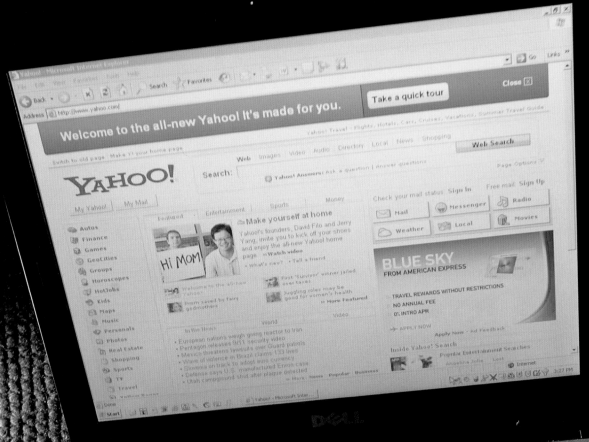

Surfing the Internet, like this man who is viewing the Yahoo website, became popular in the 1990s.

$\mathcal{W}$ITH THE WORLD WIDE WEB (WWW), YOU AND YOUR COMMUNICATION DEVICES CAN SURF YOUR WAY THROUGH ONE OF THE TRULY GREAT WONDERS OF COMMUNICATION. AT THE HEART OF THE WWW IS SOMETHING CALLED FEEDBACK. THINK ABOUT SHANNON'S BASIC COMMUNICATION MODEL. WE SHOULD ADD FEEDBACK TO THE MODEL. FEEDBACK IS WHEN THE COMMUNICATION PROCESS REPEATS ITSELF OR REVERSES. A GOOD EXAMPLE IS THE TELEPHONE. THE PERSON ON ONE TELEPHONE SAYS SOMETHING AND THEN WAITS FOR FEEDBACK FROM THE OTHER PERSON.

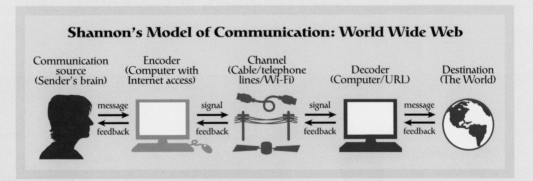

Shannon's Model of Communication: World Wide Web

Communication source (Sender's brain) — message / feedback — Encoder (Computer with Internet access) — signal / feedback — Channel (Cable/telephone lines/Wi-Fi) — signal / feedback — Decoder (Computer/URL) — message / feedback — Destination (The World)

> *"When I took office, only high energy physicists had ever heard of what is called the world wide web. Now even my cat has its own page."*
>
> —*Bill Clinton, former U.S. president, 1996*

Feedback is the backbone of the WWW. Someone sends a request. The WWW finds what it thinks the person wants. If it is not what's wanted, the person changes the topic a bit and whizzes it back to the WWW. Feedback provides connections to websites, people, and information resources. Feedback makes the WWW a powerful communication tool.

ORIGINS OF THE WORLD WIDE WEB

The WWW is a very large collection of texts, images, and videos. The Internet is the communication system for making it all possible.

In the 1960s, the U.S. Department of Defense wanted a national computer network in which one communication site could communicate with many sites. In 1969 it awarded a contract to BBN Technologies to build a network called the Advanced Research Projects Agency Network (ARPANet).

On October 29, 1969, BBN started up ARPANet. The network sent and received data related to research and national defense. ARPANet began to expand rapidly. Government agencies, research centers, universities, and businesses became network members. By September 1973, the ARPANet had forty members. The modern Internet evolved out of ARPANet.

These BBN employees who created ARPANet are photographed in the 1980s. Many of the people who worked on the project were former Massachusetts Institute of Technology (MIT) engineers.

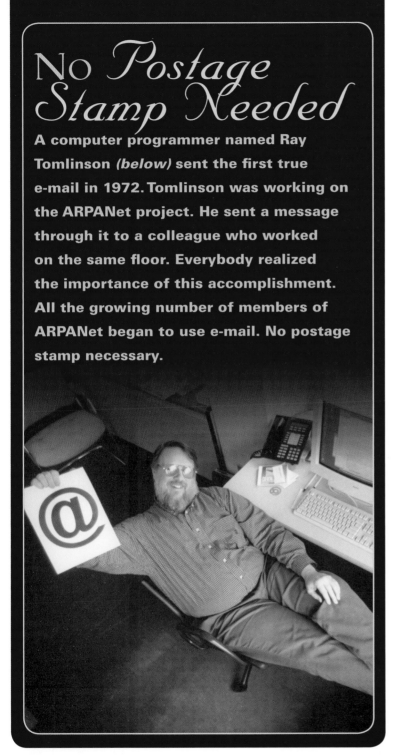
HOW THE WWW WORKS

One of the nice things about the WWW is that it works quickly, smoothly, and accurately. The user types a few words or a Web page address into a browser. A browser is software that provides access to the Web. Browsers include Internet Explorer, Foxfire, and Chrome. Behind the scenes, wonders of communication take place.

The browser begins by interpreting the uniform resource locator, or URL. The URL usually begins with http://www. This is the unique address for a file somewhere on the Internet. The URL may refer to a general website or a particular page within a website.

A user can type in the URL directly or type in a subject, for example, *media player*. Typing the exact URL will bring up a specific file. Typing in *media player* will bring a list of Web pages about media players. In either case, the browser turns the typed URL address or subject words into a basic set of numbers. The computer works these numbers to hunt down what was requested.

WHO'S IN CHARGE?

All around the Internet are computers and people whose primary job is just to keep all these computers running. They manage all the billions of Internet protocol (IP) addresses and other information needed to run the Internet.

Communication companies and Internet providers play a major role in keeping the Internet going. They include telephone, cable, and satellite companies and even some universities and government agencies. Nobody owns the Internet. Still, it involves a lot of people.

What keeps all this from turning into a big mess? People do. A number of different organizations administer Internet rules. Groups of people from different walks of life all around the world work out agreements on these policies and rules.

One example is the Internet Society (ISOC). This is a nonprofit organization that recommends Internet rules and procedures. It represents more than eighty organizations and more than twenty-eight hundred individual members. These people provide different expertise and experiences. An elected board of trustees runs the society. To gain access to the Internet, computers have to follow the rules the groups have agreed on. So there is somebody in charge!

A LOT IN *One Line*

At the heart of the URL is an IP address. The IP address tells the browser what file it wants and the best route to get there. It consists of four sets of numbers separated by periods. For example: 123.45.678.166. The computer can only work with zeros and ones, so it translates these numbers into zeros and ones. The numbers name subnetworks of computers in the Internet. A WWW request travels through subnetworks to get to the subject or specific address.

IPs are divided into domains. Organizing into domains cuts down on the search time. The domain includes:

- *.gov* (indicates a website run by a government agency)
- *.edu* (for websites associated with educational sites, such as schools and universities)
- *.org* (for websites run by nonprofit organizations)
- *.mil* (for websites run by military agencies)
- *.com* (for websites run as commercial businesses)
- *.net* (usually means networks)

WHO IS *Tim Berners-Lee?*

Physicist and computer scientist Tim Berners-Lee created the World Wide Web in 1990. It grew very quickly. By July 2008, the WWW linked more than 100 million websites. At that time, there were one trillion unique addresses on the Web. The World Wide Web has created an electronic global village in which we all live.

Berners-Lee graduated from Oxford University in Britain. He presently lives in the United States and is involved with the creation of advanced, more powerful versions of the WWW.

SOCIALIZING ON THE WWW

Social networking existed many thousands of years before computers. People socialize with neighbors, with school friends, with church groups, and in dozens of other ways. But the term has taken on the meaning of getting together on the WWW. People connect to groups for friendships, to share information, for business, and even for health reasons. Social networking stretches all around the world, involving hundreds of millions of people.

Tim Berners-Lee is credited with creating the World Wide Web.

> *"The development of the World Wide Web is a great example of human endeavor in which many people participated, driven by individual excitement and a common vision"*
>
> —*Jim Berners-Lee, developer of the World Wide Web, 2002*

Some websites are devoted to just socializing, such as Facebook, Twitter, MySpace, Classmates, and others. Software is available to help individuals design their social networking sites. Users also can express opinions and give advice on websites called blogs.

One downside to social networks is cyber bullying. Teasing and bullying have been around since humans started populating Earth. It can be nasty and potentially dangerous on the WWW. Cyber bullying allows the bullies to be anonymous. They spread threats and insults in words and images. These can travel around the world on the Internet and remain on the site for a long time. Government officials, teachers, and parents have tried to curb cyber bullying, but it is difficult to stop.

Some people worry that social networking causes people to live in an unreal world. Some networkers create fantasy lives for themselves very far from the truth. Some networkers write things about themselves they later wish they hadn't when a possible employer searches the Web for information about them. In spite of these drawbacks, social networking is entertaining and it fulfills a need to belong. It can supply users with serious and useful information as well.

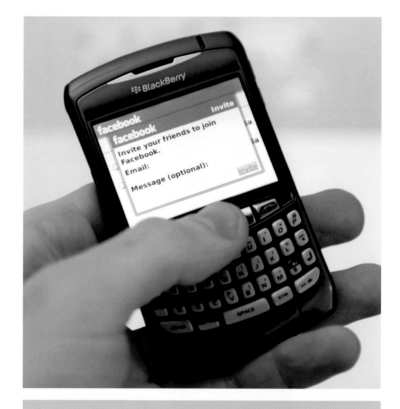

Social networking sites such as Facebook, shown here on a BlackBerry wireless handheld device, and Twitter allow users to keep in touch and express opinions over the Internet.

Internet cafés, such as this one in New York City, give people who don't have a computer or Internet access at their home a place to surf the Web.

FUTURE WONDERS

The WWW provides information, entertainment, and communication. It is destined to become even more personal and interactive as it interacts with the many different electronic devices. Scientists have even thought about attaching chips to human brains. People could have the World Wide Web directly in their heads. That would really be a wonder of communication!

New versions of the WWW are a reality. They are called Web 2.0 and Web 3.0. These newer versions have advanced high-speed power to connect to all kinds of media. They will use better methods of association.

With association, the Web figures out indirectly what other information a user might want. If someone typed in *cats and dogs,* the Web returns a list of items about cats and dogs.

Using association, the computer looks at what was typed and then goes one step further. An interest in cats and dogs may mean an interest in all kinds of pets. The computer will also send information on pets. The computer associates the idea of cats and dogs with pets. It also associates people with people. For example, it might connect a lawyer to other lawyers that practice in the same area of law.

There is a great big exciting world out there. The World Wide Web is helping to find it. Surf away!

7 Robot
COMMUNICATION

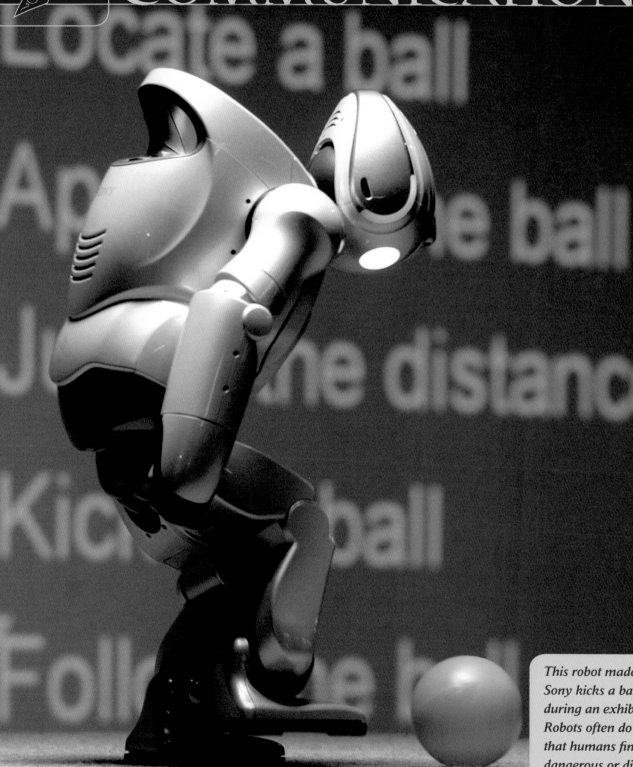

Locate a ball

Ap...e ball

Ju...he distance

Ki...ball

Foll...

This robot made by Sony kicks a ball during an exhibition. Robots often do jobs that humans find dangerous or difficult.

COMMUNICATION BETWEEN HUMANS AND ROBOTS IS THE SEVENTH WONDER OF COMMUNICATION. A FICTIONAL STORYBOOK CHARACTER NAMED DR. DOOLITTLE TALKED TO THE ANIMALS. PEOPLE ARE BEGINNING TO DO SOMETHING MORE REMARKABLE. THEY ARE TALKING TO MACHINES, AND THE MACHINES UNDERSTAND THEM!

Robots are not like those humanlike machines in the movies that think, act, and do good and evil. Real robots are not movie superstars. They are even more fascinating in their own way. Interest in robots is growing. People are seeing that they are useful in all areas of life. Robots are reliable workers, and they do what they are told.

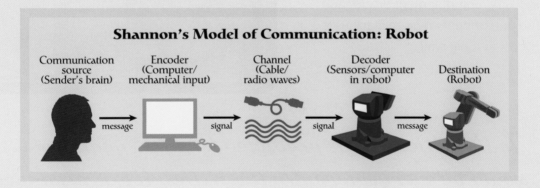

Shannon's Model of Communication: Robot

Communication source (Sender's brain) → message → Encoder (Computer/mechanical input) → signal → Channel (Cable/radio waves) → signal → Decoder (Sensors/computer in robot) → message → Destination (Robot)

What Is a Robot?

A robot is a device with mechanical parts, such as arms, legs, and sometimes a head. Robots have sensors that can tell them what's going on around them. They interact with their environments and with humans and other machines. Some robots can do some things on their own if they have been programmed to by humans. Robotics is the field that deals with designing and building robots.

Dirty, Difficult, and Dangerous Work

Robots do work that is dirty, dangerous, and difficult. Industry, law enforcement, and space exploration use robots. So does the health-care industry, entertainment world, and fire departments. The military uses robots in a big way.

Robot *Coal Miners*

Mining is still a dangerous job for humans. Engineers are developing promising technology that uses robots to aid in mining *(below)*. They can do routine work, such as digging coal and loading it on conveyors and trucks. They can also lay out explosives. The robots can help rescue workers when mining accidents occur. Researchers at Carnegie Mellon University in Pennsylvania designed a number of prototypes of mining robots. They named the first one *Groundhog* and a later one *Cave Crawler*.

"In the fifties, it was predicted that in 5 years robots would be everywhere. In the sixties, it was predicted that in 10 years robots would be everywhere. In the seventies, it was predicted that in 20 years robots would be everywhere. In the eighties, it was predicted that in 40 years robots would be everywhere."

—*Marvin Minsky, one of the fathers of artificial (computer) intelligence, n.d.*

Robots crawl through sewers, air ducts, and all kinds of dirty places to clean and inspect them. In the hospital, robots help doctors perform surgery. On the battlefield, robots fly over enemy territory. They defuse roadside bombs, rescue the wounded, and enter and survey dangerous places. In space exploration, robots crawl around the moon or a planet, taking pictures and digging to gather soil samples to analyze.

Right: *A U.S. astronaut is anchored to a robotic arm to make repairs to the International Space Station.* **Below:** *Soldiers in Iraq use the Talon robot during a military exercise. The Talon is used to defuse roadside bombs.*

A U.S. Air Force captain (below) *flies an MQ-9 Reaper* (above) *at an air base in Afghanistan, while another soldier controls the video camera.*

A KILLER
Flying Robot

The military uses robots in a number of ways. One kind of robot is a drone, an unmanned aircraft for spying and attack. The military has used drones in Afghanistan and Iraq. The MQ-9 Reaper Hunter/Killer UAV flies 300 miles (483 km) per hour, at a height of up to 50,000 feet (15,000 m). It carries deadly weapons. The drone is controlled by pilots sitting at computers, thousands of miles away, communicating via satellite and continuous video.

WHO WAS *Alan Turing?*

Alan Mathison Turing (1912–1954) was a brilliant British mathematician. Many people consider him to be the creator of the modern computer and one of the fathers of the field of artificial intelligence. Turing *(below)* worked out the basic math concepts for designing computers. He did this with his Turing machine. A Turing machine is not a real machine. It is a thought exploration of the mathematics needed to operate a computer. Engineers used his ideas when they built a real computer.

ROBOT DECISION MAKING

The source for robot communication is the human or the machines programmed by humans. To do their tasks, robots have to have the information to know what to do and how to do it.

A robot is rolling along and comes to a door. The robot has to be able to sense whether the door is open or closed. If the door is closed, the robot has a decision to make. Does it stop, does it turn, or does it crash into the door? A smart robot might be able to open the door.

The technological area that deals with the robot's decision about a closed door is known as artificial intelligence (AI). Artificial intelligence is defined as the behavior of computers or computer-driven machines that would be considered intelligent when done by living things.

For centuries, people envisioned mechanical dolls and other toys that could move and talk like humans. In modern times, they want computers that can think as well as humans or better. This is not likely to happen anytime soon, but that should not be the goal. The goal is to make machines do their tasks in the best way they can.

WAYS OF COMMUNICATING WITH ROBOTS

In Shannon's model, the robot is the receiver of communication. The robot avoided the door because it received a communication from humans. The communication involves both instructions from inside and from outside.

Robots do some things on their own following computer programs stored inside them. With the door problem, sensors might alert the robot. Then the computer inside the robot switches to the part of the program that directs the mechanical part of the robot to stop or turn.

The robot operators can also channel information to the robot with a cable. Or the operator may do it remotely with a radio-controlled device. Using direct cables for control are more reliable than a remote. But cables can get in the way if the robot moves around. A 36-million-mile (58 million km) cable is impossible if the robot is on Mars.

A common way to input a robot is with a computer. The human operator types a command or clicks an icon or a menu item. Physical gadgets, such as sensors, master arms, or joysticks also send instructions. A master arm is a device that fits on the arm and hand. When a person makes a movement with it, the robot duplicates the movement.

Computer scientists, linguists, engineers, and others are working hard to make robots that recognize voices and understand human language. Voice recognition technology converts the spoken word to computer language. With this technology, a person using a wheelchair can control it by talking to it.

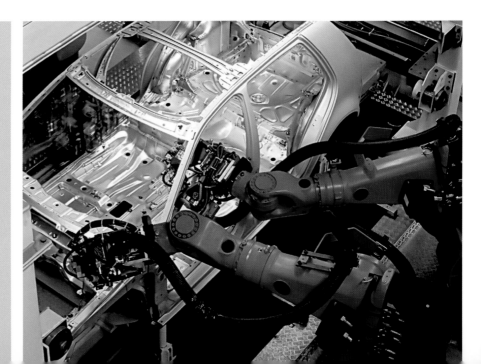

These robots build an automobile at a factory in the United States.

COMMUNICATING
WITH
Wheelchairs

Technicians can program some of the latest models of wheelchairs to go to places on demand (like the one shown above with the professors who developed it). A disabled person takes a trip to a specific location with the wheelchair, and the wheelchair remembers the path it took to get there. It can be just around the house or outside. All the user has to say is, "I want a hamburger." The wheelchair has been programmed to know how to go to the place that serves hamburgers.

FUTURE WONDERS

Will there ever be a real R2-D2, the robot in *Star Wars*? In the short time that robotics has existed, experts have accomplished many wonders. But robotics is still a very young field. An amazing future is ahead. This includes new developments in nanotechnology, advanced computers and software, and virtual reality. Virtual reality uses computers, headsets, goggles, and sensors on the skin to create an artificial environment. With these devices, a person might feel he or she is flying an airplane or skiing down Mount Everest.

Scientists are beginning to apply these tools to robots. Still, at the heart of it all will be the ability to communicate to the robots, to tell them what they should do. Dr. Dolittle talked to his animals. In the twenty-first century, people are communicating with robots. The wonders are still coming.

A FINAL WORD

We depend on communication to get through life. It is the core of our activities twenty-four hours a day. Even as we dream in our sleep, our brain is trying to tell us something. Be a great communicator in all you do.

TIMELINE

ca. 3500 B.C. Sumerians develop cuneiform writing, and Egyptians develop hieroglyphics.

ca. A.D. 104 Tsai Lun creates paper from wood fiber.

170 Parchment is made from dried reeds, and papyrus rolls are made from the papyrus plant in ancient Egypt.

305 The Chinese invent the wooden printing plate with symbols carved from a woodblock.

953 Ma'dh al-Mu'izz demands a pen that won't leak onto his hands or clothes, and the fountain pen is invented.

1041 The movable type printing press is invented in China.

ca. 1439 A metal moveable type printing press is invented by Johannes Gutenberg. The Gutenberg Bible is published in the 1450s.

1861 Paul Broca identifies the speech production center in the brain.

1876 Alexander Graham Bell invents the telephone. Bell files a patent for his device only hours before fellow inventor Elisha Gray.

1892 An automated telephone exchange from New York to Chicago is demonstrated.

1903 *The Great Train Robbery,* the first feature film, is made. Audience members are shocked and thrilled when a gun is pointed at them from onscreen.

1910 Thomas Edison demonstrates the first talking motion picture.

1927 The first TV broadcast takes place in Britain.

The first talking feature movie, *The Jazz Singer,* stars Al Jolson.

1928 Cartoon movie star Mickey Mouse is born. Mickey and girlfriend Minnie Mouse debut in the silent short *Plane Crazy.*

1937 Alan Turing proposes his Turing machine for exploring the mathematics needed to operate a computer.

1938 Laszlo Biro develops the first ballpoint pen.

1946 The ENIAC, the first fully electronic computer, is built at the University of Pennsylvania.

1957 Noam Chomsky publishes *Syntactic Structures,* his first major contribution to the scientific study of language.

1958 Jack Kilby and Robert Noyce both invent the integrated circuit.

1968 Alan Kay envisions a "personal, portable" computer, leading to the development of the laptop.

1969 ARPANet, the ancestor to the Internet, is developed by the U.S. Department of Defense.

1971 IBM releases the first commercially available floppy disk.

1976 Apple introduces a small personal computer.

1981 IBM sells the company's first PC.

1990 Tim Berners-Lee develops the World Wide Web.

1998 Larry Page and Sergey Brin invent Google while at Stanford University in California.

2004 The social website Facebook is launched. "Micro-blogging" site Twitter is founded two years later.

2008 Web 2.0, the second generation of web design and development, becomes operational with greater interactivity for users. 3G wireless communication also increases in popularity, allowing users access to more information at faster speeds.

2009 Television goes digital across the United States. Germany, Sweden, Switzerland, and other European countries converted to digital television in 2006 and 2007.

CHOOSE AN EIGHTH WONDER

Now that you've read about the Seven Wonders of Communication, do a little research to choose an eighth wonder. How about getting your friends involved in this? Communicate!

One subject might be animal communication. Check online and in the library to find out about amazing examples of animal communication. Maybe you would want to find out more about
- *Insect communication*
- *Reptile communication*
- *Bird communication*
- *Mammal communication*
- *How animals communicate with humans*

You might even try gathering photos and writing your own chapter on the eighth wonder.

GLOSSARY

blog: a website that is frequently updated with news, events, and personal comments

feedback: information that goes back and forth among people, among people and machines, or among machines for continuing modification

global positioning systems (GPS): a navigation system that uses signals beamed back and forth from satellite to Earth to locate a physical object

larynx: an organ in the throat, often called the voice box, that uses air from the lungs to help produce speech

nanotechnology: developing materials or devices at the atomic and molecular levels

neuroanatomist: a scientist who studies the brain to find out where specific functions are located and how they are carried out

palate: the roof of the mouth

papyrus plant: a grasslike plant processed by the ancient Egyptians to use as writing material

photojournalism: the use of photography to tell a story or report events, usually with accompanying text

prototype: an original example or model that serves as a guide for later stages of development

qubit: an information unit in quantum computing

real time: the actual time that an action is taken, not at a later time

sensors: devices that detect physical conditions in the environment and convert them to a signal for a robot

virtual reality: computer-based technology that allows humans to interact with a real or imagined situation, for example, a flight training simulator

wireless: electronic communication without the use of wires to connect devices

SOURCE NOTES

12   Noam Chomsky, *Language and the Mind,* 3rd ed. (Cambridge, MA: MIT Press, 2006), 88.

13   Wikipedia, "Wendell Phillips," *Wikipedia,* 2008, http://en.wikipedia.org/wiki/Wendell_Phillips (December 20, 2008).

20   Telephone Tribute, "Telephone Trivia and Quotes," *telephonetribute.com,* 2006, http://www.telephonetribute.com/telephonetrivia.html (December 20, 2008).

21   Telephone Tribute, "Telephone Trivia and Quotes," *telephonetribute.com,* 2006, http://www.telephonetribute.com/telephonetrivia.html (December 20, 2008).

32   Ken Rockwell, "Your Camera Does Not Matter," *KenRockwell.com,* 2008, http://www.kenrockwell.com/tech/notcamera.htm (December 20, 2008).

36   Quote Garden, "Quotations about Television," *QuoteGarden.com,* 2007, http://www.quotegarden.com/television.html (December 20, 2008).

38   Quote Garden, "Quotations about Television," *QuoteGarden.com,* 2007, http://www.quotegarden.com/television.html (December 20, 2008).

41   Quote Garden, "Quotations about Television," *QuoteGarden.com,* 2007, http://www.quotegarden.com/television.html (December 20, 2008).

50   BrainyMedia.com.com, "Bill Gates," *BrainyQuotes,* 2008, http://www.brainyquote.com/quotes/quotes/b/billgates191234.html (December 20, 2008).

56   Bill Clinton, 2002, "Bill Clinton Quotes," *Funny Quotes,* http://www.amusingquotes.com/h/c/Bill_Clinton_1.htm (April 8, 2009).

60   Tim Berners-Lee, "The World Wide Web—Past Present and Future," *Japan Prize Commemorative Lecture, 2002,* http://www.w3.org/2002/04/Japan/Lecture.html (April 8, 2009).

64   Museum of Modern Heritage, "Marvin Minsky," *Quotes about Robots,* 2006, http://www.moah.org/exhibits/archives/robotman/quotes/quotes.html (December 20, 2008).

SELECTED BIBLIOGRAPHY

Alesso, H. Peter, and Craig F. Smith. *Thinking on the Web: Berners-Lee, Gödel, and Turing.* Hoboken, NJ: John Wiley and Sons, 2008.

Baker, Christopher W. *Robots among Us: The Challenges and Promises of Robotics.* Brookfield, CT: Milbrook Press, 2002.

Campbell, Marc. *Digital Photography for Teens.* Boston: Course PTR, 2007.

Castells, Manuel. *Mobile Communication and Society: A Global Perspective.* Cambridge, MA: MIT Press, 2007.

Chomsky, Noam. *On Nature and Language.* New York: Cambridge University Press, 2002.

Golbeck, Jennifer. *Trust on the World Wide Web: A Survey.* Boston: Now Publishers, 2008.

Gralla, Preston. *The Complete Idiot's Guide to Cool Ways to Communicate Online.* Indianapolis: Alpha Books, 2000.

Harris, Frances Jackson. *I Found It on the Internet: Coming of Age Online.* Chicago: American Library Association, 2005.

Hyland, Tony. *How Robots Work.* North Mankato, MN: Smart Apple Media, 2008.

McFedries, Paul. *Computers Simplified.* Hoboken, NJ: John Wiley and Sons, 2007.

FURTHER READING AND WEBSITES

Books

Childress, Diana. *Johannes Gutenberg and the Printing Press.* Minneapolis: Twenty-First Century Books, 2008. This narrative describes Gutenberg's invention and discusses how it changed the world.

Domaine, Helena. *Robotics.* Minneapolis: Lerner Publications Company, 2006. This book in the Cool Science series looks at robotics from ancient legends to modern technology.

Goranson, Christopher D. *Everything You Need to Know about Misinformation on the Internet.* New York: Rosen, 2002. Know what's going on in the chat rooms, newsgroups, and blogs and how to play it safe with e-mail.

Jones, David. *Mighty Robots: Mechanical Marvels That Fascinate and Frighten.* Toronto: Annick Press, 2005. Jones discusses how robotics developed, how robots do their jobs, and how robots are used in the movies and in books. An interesting discussion of the challenges of using artificial intelligence to communicate with robots is included.

Lensinski, Jeanne. *Bill Gates.* Minneapolis: Twenty-First Century Books, 2009. This is a biography of the man who developed much of the top-selling software for PCs.

McPherson, Stephanie Sammartino. *Tim Berners-Lee: Inventor of the World Wide Web.* Minneapolis: Twenty-First Century Books, 2010. Learn more about the man behind what we now know as the World Wide Web.

Miller, Ron. *Digital Art.* Minneapolis: Twenty-First Century Books, 2008. Digital art is all around us—especially on television and the Internet. This book gives information on the history of digital art, as well as what a digital artist does.

——. *Robot Explorers.* Minneapolis: Twenty-First Century Books, 2008. Learn about the unmanned missions throughout the solar system, from the first lunar and planetary probes of the 1960s up to the recent sophisticated Mars rover missions.

Mullins, Lisa. *Inventing the Printing Press.* New York: Crabtree Publisher. 2007. For centuries many people, from many parts of the world, tried different ways to print the written word and images. Read about some of these adventures.

Richter, Joanne. *Inventing the Camera.* New York: Crabtree Publisher, 2006. No one person invented the camera, although there were highlight events. This book tells the history of cameras, and it also gives some pointers on how to take good pictures.

Woods, Michael, and Mary B. Woods. *Ancient Communication: From Grunts to Graffiti.* Minneapolis: Twenty-First Century Books, 2000. This book starts with how ancient peoples solved the problem of communication—and follows communication to modern alphabets and universal languages.

——. *The History of Communication.* Minneapolis: Lerner Publications Company, 2006. The authors take readers through inventions that have changed communication throughout history, including the printing press, telephone, television, and the Internet.

Websites

Communication Devices of the Future

htttp://www.forbes.com/2005/10/20/cx_gd_1024featslide_comm05.html

This is a neat website with short videos and text about communication devices that are coming into existence. It includes such things as micromedia players, powerful but inexpensive laptop computers, voice over the Internet devices, bio-identification chips that we carry around, and many other things.

The History of the Computer: First PC's and the Future Computer Timeline

http://www.superwarehouse.com/blog/2008/09/history-of-computer-first-pcs-and_2477.html

This is a blog that has some interesting comments and pictures related to the history of PCs and on what might be down the road.

HowStuffWorks

http://www.howstuffworks.com/

This website is loaded with explanations of how things work, including telephones, DNA computers, televisions, cameras, and many other things. There are a lot of photos, and the descriptions are easy to understand.

NASA

http://www.nasa.gov/

The National Aeronautics and Space Administration is involved in communications in many ways. This site shows many of the agency's communication activities. It is a fascinating website.

What Is Web 2.0

http://www.oreillynet.com/pub/a/oreilly/tim/news/2005/09/30/what-is-web-20.html

This website explains the difference between the original WWW and Web 2.0. It has an interesting table that compares the two versions side by side.

INDEX

ABOUT THE AUTHOR

Donald Cleveland is professor emeritus, Department of Library and Information Sciences, the University of North Texas. His specialty areas include information science and communication technology. He has served as a consultant on information and communication systems for both national and international organizations. He and his wife, Ana, have traveled extensively in the United States and many other countries for leisure and for professional purposes.

PHOTO ACKNOWLEDGMENTS

TThe images in this book are used with the permission of: © Laura Westlund/Independent Picture Service, pp. 5 (top), 7, 9, 17, 27, 31, 35, 43, 55, 63; © Alfred Eisenstaedt/Time & Life Pictures/Getty Images, p. 5 (bottom); © age fotostock/SuperStock, pp. 6, 33, 47 (bottom), 48; AP Photo/Murad Sezer, p. 8; © Hulton Archive/Getty Images, p. 10; © iStockphoto.com/Jason Walton, p. 11; The Art Archive/Museo Provincial de Bellas Artes Salamanca/Gianni Dagli Orti, p. 12; © Paul Popper/Popperfoto/Getty Images, p. 13; © Rischgitz/Hulton Archive/Getty Images, p. 15 (top); © Huntington Library/SuperStock, p. 15 (bottom); Library of Congress, pp. 16 (LC-DIG-matpc-08799), 26 (LC-USZ62-35617), 29 (top, LC-DIG-cwpbh-03798), 36 (LC-USZ62-77563); © Popperfoto/Getty Images, p. 18; © Topical Press Agency/Hulton Archive/Getty Images, p. 19; © SSPL/The Image Works, p. 21 (top, and center right); © Authenticated News/Hulton Archive/Getty Images, p. 21 (center left); © iStockphoto.com/Christoph Ermel, p. 21 (bottom); © Randy Allbritton/Photodisc/Getty Images, p. 22; © Olesiaru/Dreamstime.com, p. 23 (left); © Phlens/Dreamstime.com, p. 23 (right); © Erik Simonsen/ Photographer's Choice/Getty Images, p. 24; © STEPHANE DE SAKUTIN/AFP/Getty Images, p. 25; © Todd Strand/Independent Picture Service, p. 28 (top); © Travelpix Ltd/Photographer's Choice/Getty Images, pp. 28 (bottom), 72 (center right); National Archives, p. 29 (bottom, 111-BZ-11); Edison/The Kobal Collection, p. 30; © NASA/JPL-Caltech/University of Arizona/Getty Images, p. 32; © H. Armstrong Roberts/Retrofile/Getty Images, pp. 34, 72 (bottom right); © iStockphoto.com/Grafissimo, p. 38; © A. Chederros/ONOKY/Getty Images, p. 39; © PAUL J. RICHARDS/AFP/Getty Images, p. 40; AP Photo/Jae C. Hong, p. 41; Courtesy of the Computer History Museum, pp. 42, 44 (top), 45 (top); © Topham/The Image Works, p. 44 (bottom); © Andersen Ross/Digital Vision/Getty Images, p. 45 (bottom); © Jozsef Szasz - Fabian/Dreamstime.com, p. 47 (top); © Stefan Sollfors/CORBIS, p. 49; © Doug Wilson/CORBIS, p. 50; Courtesy of Apple, p. 51 (left); © David McNew/Getty Images, p. 51 (top right); © Mauritius/SuperStock, p. 51 (bottom right); © James Lauritz/ Digital Vision/Getty Images, p. 52; © Science Source/Photo Researchers, Inc., p. 53; © Justin Sullivan/Getty Images, p. 54; Courtesy Bolt, Beranek & Newman, p. 56; © Ed Quinn/CORBIS, p. 57; © CERN/SSPL/The Image Works, p. 59; © Oleksiy Maksymenko/Alamy, p. 60; © Chris Hondros/Newsmakers/Getty Images, p. 61; © PRAKASH SINGH/AFP/Getty Images, p. 62; Reprinted with permission of Carnegie Mellon University, Pittsburgh, Pennsylvania, www.cmu.edu, p. 64; NASA, p. 65 (top); Photo Courtesy of U.S. Army, Cheryl Rodewig, p. 65 (bottom); U.S. Air Force photo/Staff Sgt. Brian Ferguson, p. 66 (top); U.S. Air Force photo/Staff Sgt. James L. Harper Jr., p. 66 (bottom); © Life Magazine/Time & Life Pictures/Getty Images, p. 67; © iStockphoto.com/Ricardo Azoury, p. 68; Patrick Gillooly/MIT, p. 69; © iStockphoto.com/Brian Chan, p. 72 (top left); © Junko Kimura/Getty Images, p. 72 (top right); © Bettmann/CORBIS, p. 72 (center left); © Big Cheese Photo/SuperStock, p. 72 (bottom center); © iStockphoto.com/Oliver Malms, p. 72 (bottom left).

Front Cover: © Junko Kimura/Getty Images (top left); © Big Cheese Photo/SuperStock (top center); © iStockphoto.com/Oliver Malms (top right); © Travelpix Ltd/Photographer's Choice/Getty Images (center); © H. Armstrong Roberts/Retrofile/Getty Images (bottom left); © iStockphoto.com/Brian Chan (bottom center); © Bettmann/CORBIS (bottom right).